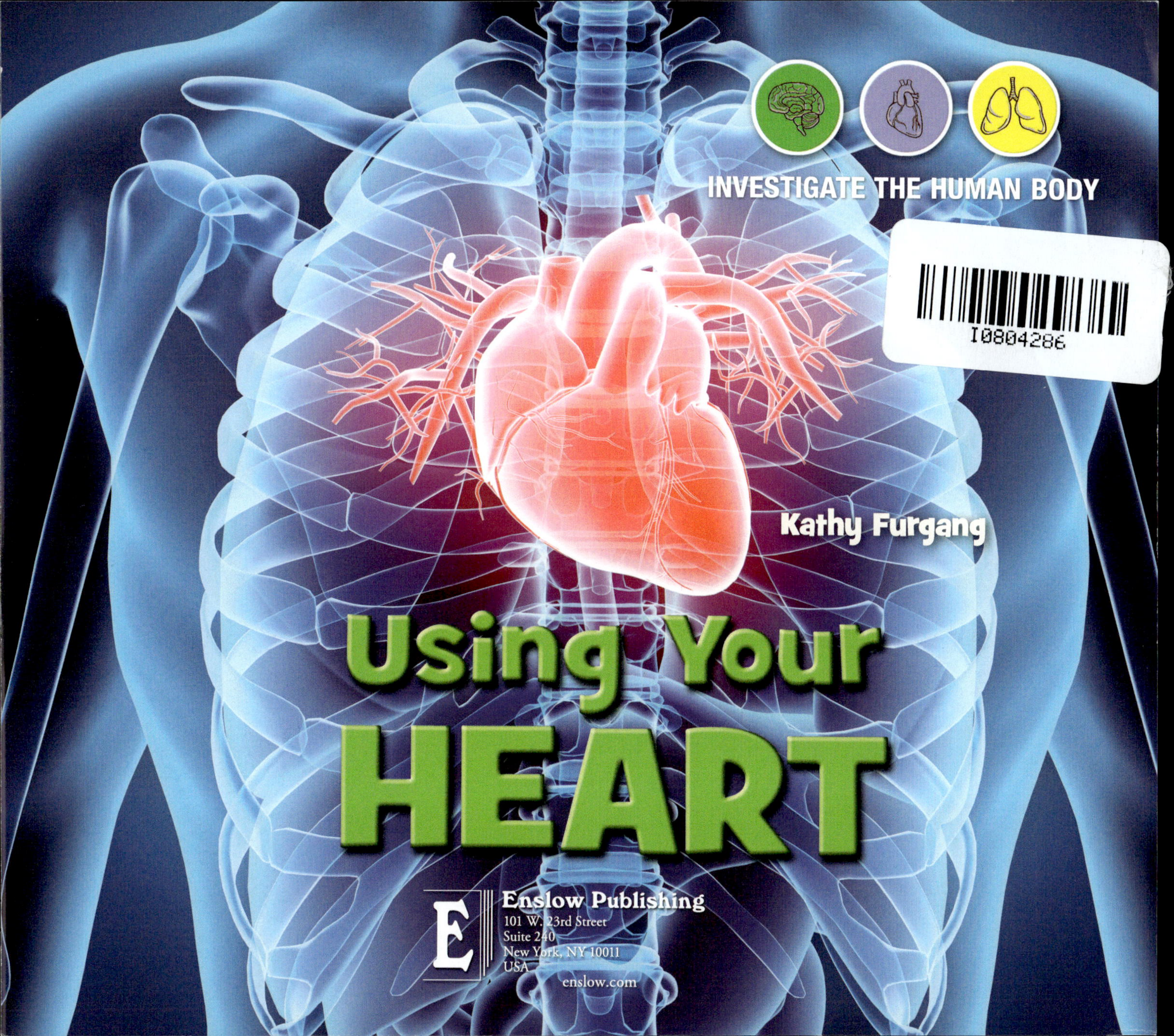

INVESTIGATE THE HUMAN BODY

Kathy Furgang

Using Your HEART

Enslow Publishing
101 W. 23rd Street
Suite 240
New York, NY 10011
USA
enslow.com

Words to Know

artery A blood vessel that carries blood away from the heart.

atria Two smaller left and right chambers of the heart. They are at the top of the heart.

blood vessels Tubes that carry blood throughout the body.

chamber A part of the heart.

circulatory system The body system that moves blood through the body and helps get rid of waste in blood.

nutrient A substance the body needs to grow and stay healthy.

oxygen A gas in the air and body that is needed for living and breathing.

valve A structure in the heart that opens and closes to keep blood flowing in the right direction through the body.

vein A blood vessel that carries blood to the heart.

ventricles Two larger left and right chambers of the heart. They are at the bottom of the heart.

Contents

Words to Know 2

How We Use the Heart 4

Parts of the Heart 8

The Heart and
Circulatory System 12

Treat Your Heart Right 17

Activity: Listen to the
Beat of Your Heart 22

Learn More 24

Index 24

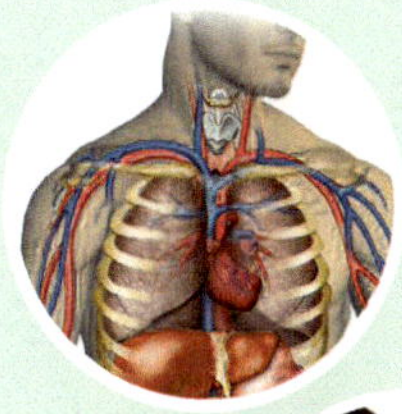

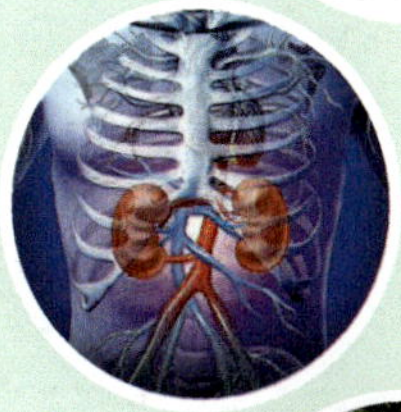

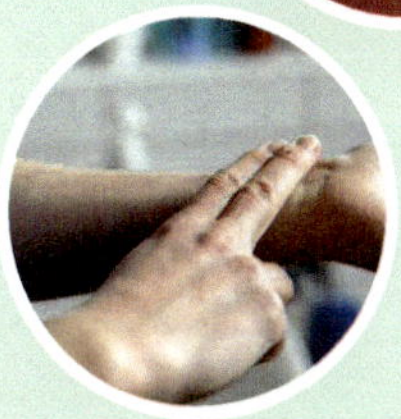

How We Use the Heart

Have you ever heard the phrase "follow your heart?" Have you heard the words "heartbreak" or "heartache?" Long ago, people thought emotions were controlled by the heart. That's because the heart beats faster during emotional times. Now we know that it is the brain—not the heart—that controls emotions.

The heart's job is to pump blood through the body. Your blood contains all of the **nutrients** your body needs to live and grow. Your blood even carries away waste. Every beat of blood through your heart keeps you alive and healthy.

Your heart plays a key role in keeping you healthy.

Your heart beats faster when you are excited.

Feel the Beat

An adult's heart beats about 60 times each minute. That is about 3,600 times an hour, or 3.5 billion times in a lifetime.

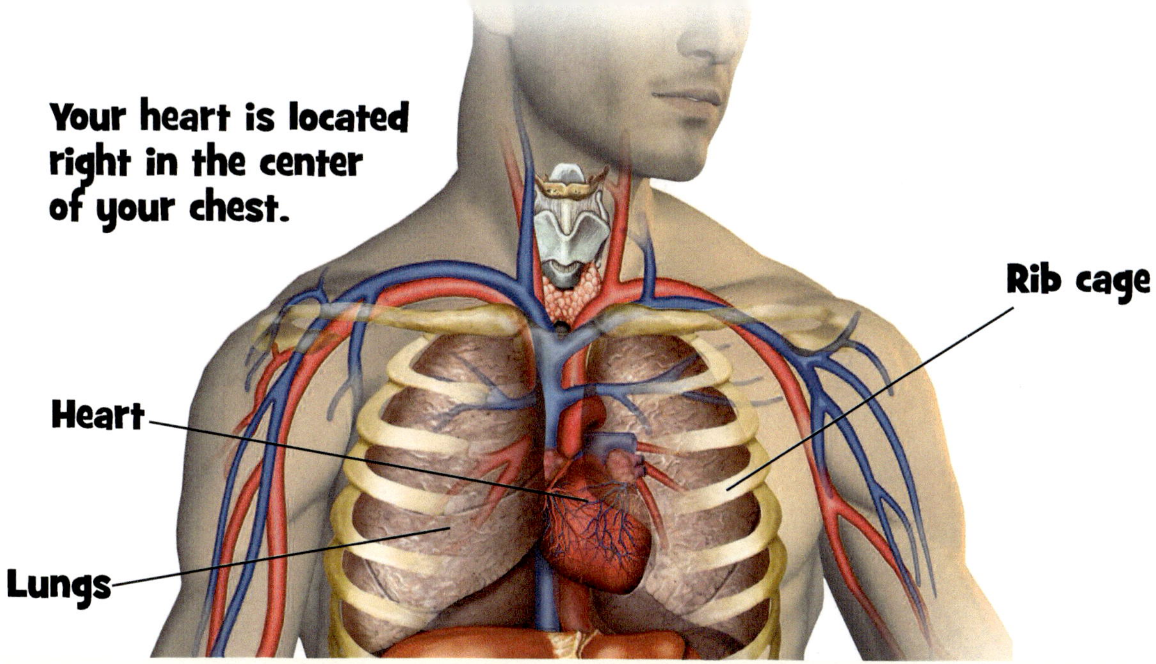

An Important Muscle

Your heart is a muscle. It is located in the center of your chest. It sits in front of your lungs and is protected by your rib cage. Your heart is only about the size of your fist. It beats, or pumps, nonstop, and you don't even have to think about it. Your body is like a machine that does thousands of important tasks. A child's heart beats about 90 times per minute.

As the heart beats, it sends a gas called **oxygen** to the rest of your body. You need this oxygen to stay healthy, alert, and alive.

Parts of the Heart

Look closely at the diagram of the heart on the next page. You can see four parts. They are called **chambers**. The two large chambers at the bottom are called **ventricles**. There is one ventricle on the left and one on the right. The two smaller chambers above them are called **atria**. There is one atrium on the left and one on the right. Blood moves through the chambers. The blood moves in the same order, over and over again. Small **valves** open and close as the blood pumps through the heart. This helps make sure the blood flows in the right direction with each beat.

YOUR HEART

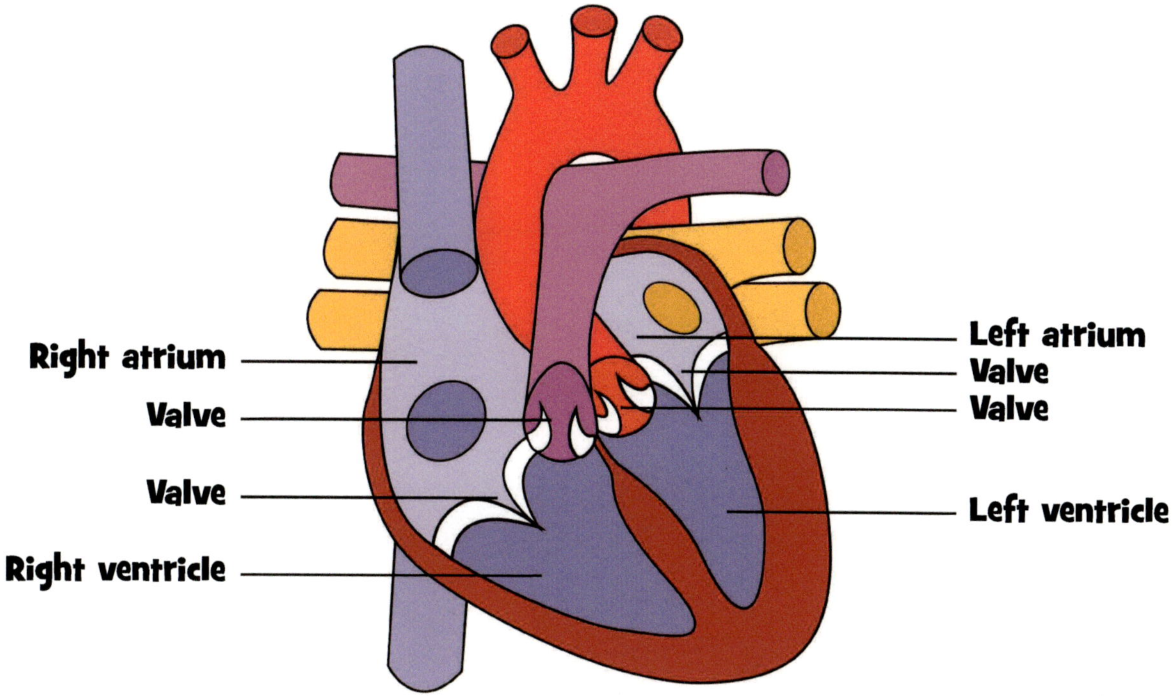

This diagram shows a view of the heart looking at the body. Notice that the left chambers are on the right and the right chambers are on the left.

The "lub-DUB" sound that the heart makes can be heard through a tool called a stethoscope.

Working Hard

Even while resting, heart muscles work twice as hard as a runner's leg muscles do while sprinting.

Blood and Oxygen on the Move

Have you ever heard your own heartbeat? The heart makes a "lub-DUB" sound over and over. That is the sound of heart valves opening and closing to move blood through the four chambers.

But how does oxygen get into your blood in the first place? It comes from the air you breathe into your lungs. This is why the heart is so close to the lungs. Oxygen passes through tiny openings from your lungs to your heart. From there, the blood travels all the way through your body.

The Heart and Circulatory System

The heart and lungs are part of the **circulatory system**. This system moves blood, oxygen, and nutrients around the body. Look at the diagram of the circulatory system on the next page. The red and blue lines show your **blood vessels**. They carry blood through the body.

Each red blood vessel shows an **artery**. An artery moves blood that's rich with oxygen away from the heart to the rest of the body. Along the way, blood loses oxygen.

Each blue blood vessel shows a **vein**. A vein moves blood from places around your body toward your heart. There, it can receive more oxygen.

CIRCULATORY SYSTEM

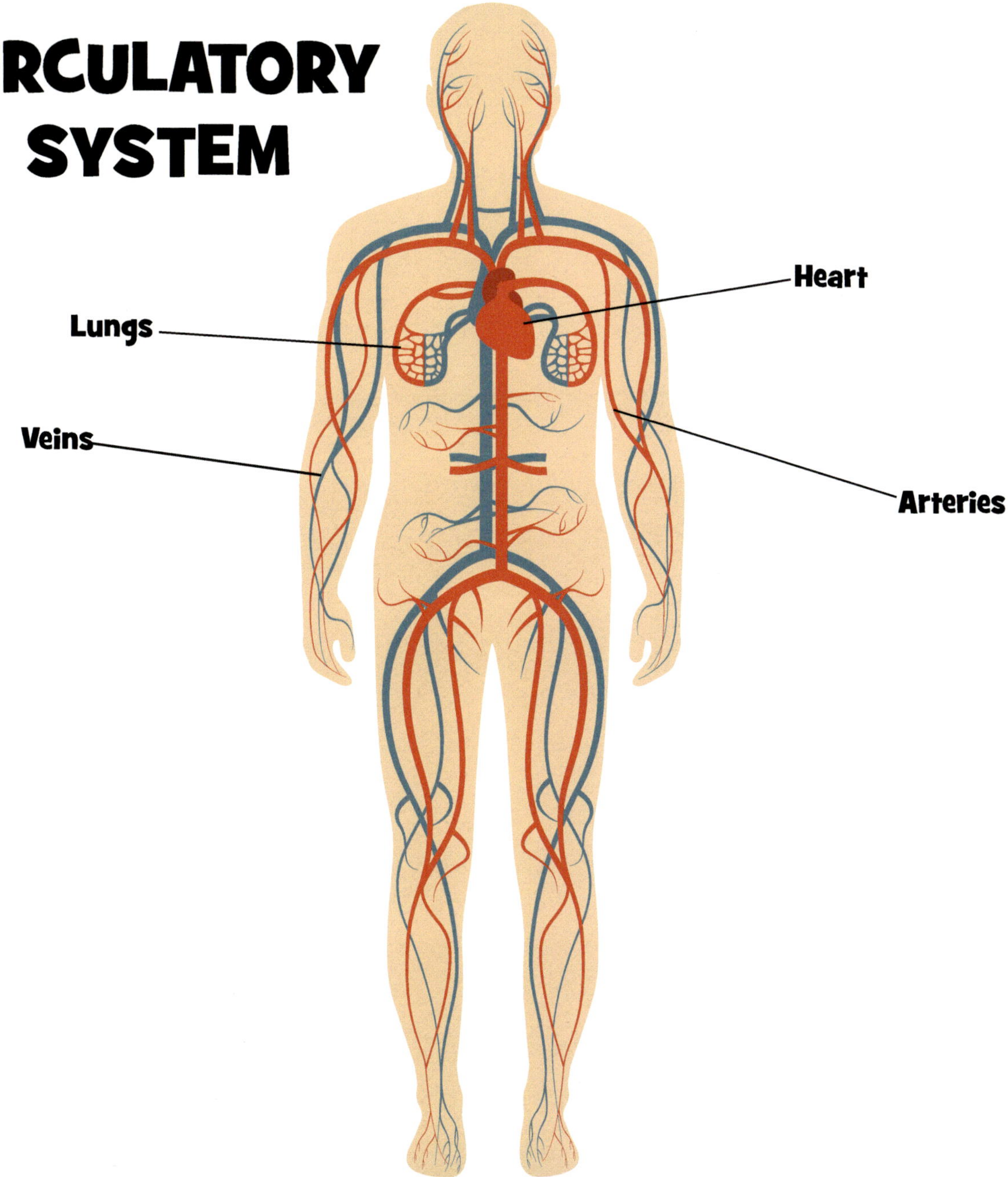

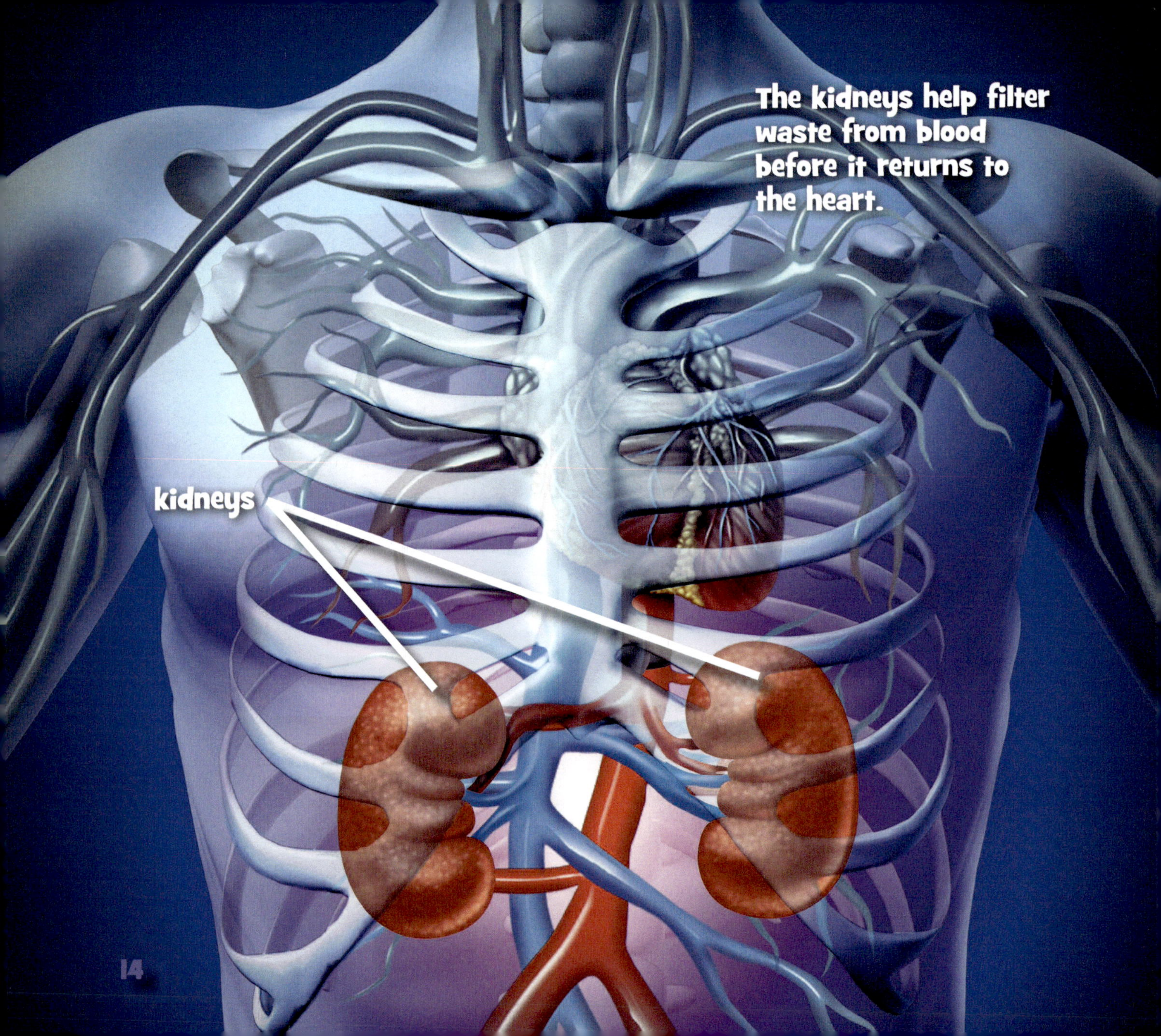
The kidneys help filter waste from blood before it returns to the heart.
kidneys

The left side of the heart gets blood from the lungs. It pumps the blood out to the rest of the body. The right side of the heart gets blood from the body. It pumps the blood to the lungs.

Going Far

In one minute, your blood pumps all the way through your body three times. In a single day, that's about 12,000 miles (19,300 kilometers), or four times across the United States!

A Long Journey through the Body

The circulatory system gets its name because the same blood circles around the body all the time. That means it moves around and around in the same path. As it moves, blood picks up waste from the foods we eat. In order to get rid of this waste, our kidneys clean the blood before it returns to the heart. The blood gets back to the heart just in time to be refreshed with more oxygen.

Treat Your Heart Right

There's no question that the heart and circulatory system keep us alive. Some doctors study and treat problems of the heart. Diseases of the heart can cause lots of problems. Sometimes a heart valve might not work well. It might not allow the heart to pump blood as strongly as it should. Diseases of the blood can also affect the heart.

Heart disease can make a person feel sick. A person might not be able to exercise to keep the heart strong. Your doctor makes sure your heart is healthy.

Heart disease is not as common in children as it is in adults.

Exercise for Heart Health

You have probably heard that exercise is good for your heart. Exercise makes your heart stronger. It pumps blood through your body faster than when you are at rest. When you breathe quickly, you take in more air and oxygen. When your heart beats faster, it quickly sends more oxygen throughout your body.

Exercise that makes your heart beat faster is good for your health. Running, walking, swimming, and team sports can make your heart strong and healthy.

Team sports are a great way to exercise with friends.

A good diet keeps the heart and circulatory system healthy.

A Happy Heart

Exercise does more than just strengthen your heart. Exercise also makes your brain release chemicals that make you feel good.

Eat for Heart Health

The foods you eat every day can also affect your heart. Fruits, vegetables, and foods high in fiber are good for your heart. They help you stay at a healthy weight. When a person is at a healthy weight, the heart does not have to pump as hard to exercise or do everyday tasks.

So, it makes sense to follow your heart. It makes even more sense to protect your heart by eating right and exercising!

Activity: Listen to the Beat of Your Heart

You will need: A timer or clock with a second hand

You can feel your heart beat by placing your hand over it. You can also feel the blood pulse through your veins. Quietly place two fingers on your wrist or the side of your neck. Feel your pulse. Each beat of your pulse equals a beat of your heart.

To see how your heartbeat changes with exercise, try this activity with the chart on page 23. For each activity, count your heartbeat or pulse for 20 seconds. Use a timer or clock to keep track. (You can jog in place for the activity.) Record your results.

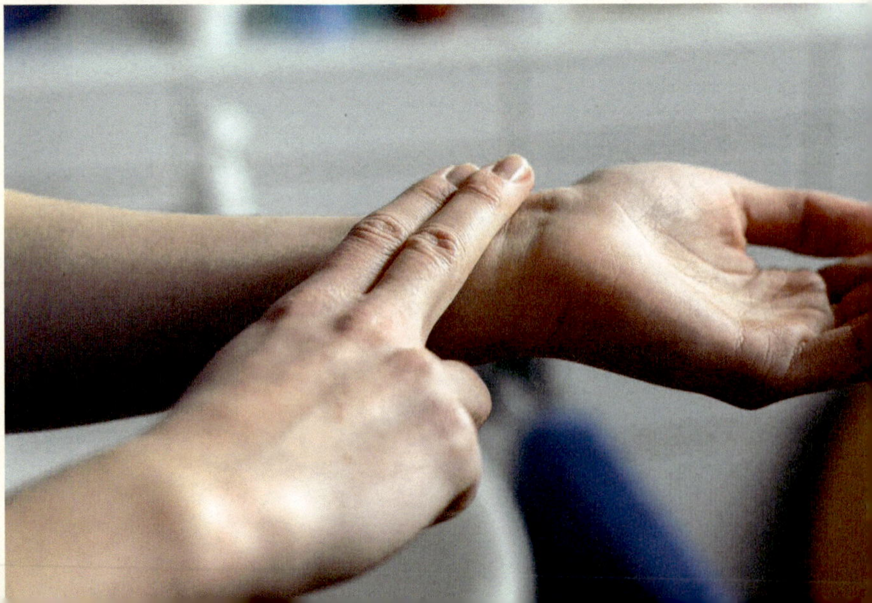

After the activity, write notes about how you felt after each step.

My Pulse at Rest and After Exercise

	Heartbeat or pulse for 20 seconds	Notes
1. At rest		
2. After jogging for 3 minutes		
3. After resting for 3 minutes		
4. After jogging for 5 minutes		
5. After resting for 5 minutes		

Learn More

Books

Canavan, Thomas. *Fit and Healthy: Heart, Lungs, and Hormones*. New York, NY: PowerKids Press, 2015.

Kenney, Karen. *Circulatory System*. Minneapolis, MN: Pogo, 2017.

Spilsbury, Richard. *The Science of the Heart and Circulatory System*. New York, NY: Gareth Stevens, 2017.

Websites

DK find out! Human Body

www.dkfindout.com/uk/human-body/

Click on "Heart and blood" to learn more about the heart and circulatory system.

Health Powered Kids

healthpoweredkids.org/

Find activities to help you make good choices about your health.

Index

arteries 12
atria 8
blood 4, 8, 11, 12, 15, 16, 17, 19, 22
blood vessels 12
chambers 8, 11
circulatory system 12, 16, 17
disease 17
exercise 17, 19, 21, 22
kidneys 16
lungs 7, 11, 12, 15
nutrients 4, 12
oxygen 7, 11, 12, 16, 19
pulse 22
rib cage 7
valves 8, 11, 17
veins 12, 22
ventricles 8

Published in 2020 by Enslow Publishing, LLC
101 W. 23rd Street, Suite 240, New York, NY 10011

Library of Congress Cataloging-in-Publication Data

Names: Furgang, Kathy, author.

Title: Using your heart / Kathy Furgang.

Description: New York : Enslow Publishing, 2020. | Series: Investigate the human body | Audience: Grade K-4. | Includes bibliographical references and index.

Identifiers: LCCN 2019013451| ISBN 9781978512832 (library bound) | ISBN 9781978512818 (paperback) | ISBN 9781978512825 (6 pack)

Subjects: LCSH: Heart--Juvenile literature.

Classification: LCC QP111.6 .F874 2020 | DDC 612.1/7--dc23

LC record available at https://lccn.loc.gov/2019013451

Printed in the United States of America

To Our Readers: We have done our best to make sure all website addresses in this book were active and appropriate when we went to press. However, the author and the publisher have no control over and assume no liability for the material available on those websites or on any websites they may link to. Any comments or suggestions can be sent by email to customerservice@enslow.com.

Photos Credits: Using Your Heart – Research by Bruce Donnola

Cover, p. 1 MDGRPHCS/Shutterstock.com; pp. 3, 7 ilusmedical/Shutterstock.com; pp. 3, 10 K2 PhotoStudio/Shutterstock.com; pp. 3, 14 Lightspring/Shutterstock.com; pp. 3, 19 Sergey Novikov/Shutterstock.com; pp. 3, 22 michaelheim/Shutterstock.com; pp. 5, 20 Syda Productions/Shutterstock.com; p. 6 Dmytro Aksonov/E+/Getty Images; p. 9 paveugra/iStock/Getty Images; p. 13 eveleen/Shutterstock.com; p. 18 Tetra Images/Alamy Stock Photo; cover graphics blackpencil/Shutterstock.com.